# Animals of South America

Dalmatian
**KIDS**

The DALMATIAN KIDS name and logo are trademarks of
Dalmatian Publishing Group, Atlanta, Georgia 30329.

Published by Dalmatian Kids, an imprint of Dalmatian Publishing Group.
Text Copyright © 2007 by Dalmatian Publishing Group, LLC
Art Copyright © 2007 Edizioni Larus S.p.A.

Printed in the U.S.A.  •  ISBN: 1-40373-240-X
07 08 09 B&M 9 8 7 6 5 4 3 2 1

# Amazon Rainforest

Spider Monkey

Brocket Deer

Antea[t]

Tapir

The Amazon rainforest of South America is the largest rainforest in the world. It covers an area the size of the United States! It is home to a huge variety of plants and animals found nowhere else on Earth.

The animals of the rainforest live not only along the ground, but also in every level of *vegetation* (plant life) up to the very treetops. This top layer forms a shady canopy which can be 165 feet above the ground.

The forest floor is home to animals that eat the leaves and grasses of the undergrowth, such as the brocket deer and the tapir. Anteaters and armadillos feed on insects, like ants and termites, while several kinds of monkeys eat the plentiful fruits. The brightly colored birds of the rainforest eat berries, seeds, nuts, and nectar from flowers. There are also *carnivorous* (meat-eating) predators of the rainforest, such as the powerful boa constrictor, and the graceful and beautiful jaguar.

Squirrel Monkey

Jaguar

Tamarin

Greenwing Macaw

Howler Monkey

Toucan

Boa Constrictor

Armadillo

Hummingbird

3

# Jaguar

The jaguar is the largest cat in the Americas. It can weigh up to 265 pounds! A jaguar's coat is yellow, covered with dark spots that are different on every animal. With its stocky body and short limbs, the jaguar can move with ease in the vast, marshy forest. It's a skilled tree climber and excellent swimmer.

Females usually have two or three cubs in a thicket. Cubs stay with their mother until they are two years old, learning how to hunt for food—and how to chase monkeys and sloths without falling from the treetops!

## What does it eat?
Large and small mammals, fish, reptiles, and eggs. It often drags its meal up a tree—away from other hungry animals.

# aguarundi

The jaguarundi belongs to the *feline* family (like housecats, lions, and jaguars), although it looks like a weasel. It weighs –17 pounds, and its body is about 22–30 inches long. Its ong tail can be another 24 inches! The jaguarundi's hort, thick legs allow it to run and slip etween the thick bushes. Its color aries, and may be blackish, silver-ray, or reddish-brown, blending with swampy, brushy vegetation.

The jaguarundi is a skillful hunter. It feeds n rodents, rabbits, birds, frogs, fish, and even oisonous snakes. The jaguarundi will also raid hicken coops, making it unpopular with chicken armers. But rice farmers like having jaguarundis around—they eat the ats that feed on their crop.

**Creature Feature:**
Like all cats, the jaguarundi likes to keep clean and often licks its fur. Unlike the housecat, it keeps its tail stretched out while washing.

# Monkeys

The Amazon rainforest is filled with an amazing variety of monkeys! Spider monkeys and little squirrel monkeys swing through the treetops like gymnasts. The big howler monkeys, the largest in the Americas, send out loud screams that can be heard as far as three miles away. The thick mane of the tiny tamarin makes this monkey quite distinctive.

Most monkeys eat nuts, fruit, leaves, and flowers, though some will also eat eggs, insects, and small reptiles.

Squirrel Monkey

Spider Monkey

Howler Monkey

Tamarin

# loth

The sloth is a fascinating animal. It hangs upside down from trees with its huge claws, moving s-l-o-w-l-y from branch to branch in search of leaves, flowers, and fruit to eat. It weighs 9–11 pounds, is about 2 feet long, and is covered with thick hair, which grows from its belly "down" to its back. This allows it to shed the rain as it hangs upside down from the branches.

The color of the sloth's hair varies from yellowish-brown to gray—but it often looks green! That's because the hairs have tiny grooves in which green algae grows. The green color of the algae helps the sloth blend in with the green leaves.

## Did You Know?

Sloths cannot stand up on the ground. When they come down from the trees, they drag themselves over the ground by grasping roots and pulling themselves forward.

## Creature Feature:
A sloth sleeps about 15 hours a day!

# Giant Anteater

The giant anteater has a very long snout that ends in a small mouth—perfect for inserting into long termite and ant tunnels! It is medium-sized—about 4 feet long and 80 pounds—and has a beautiful tail of long, bushy hair.

The anteater's sense of smell is 40 times stronger than that of a human's. It smells out the nests of ants and termites, tears open the nest walls with its powerful claws, and dips in its sticky 40-inch tongue, which it then withdraws covered with insects. A giant anteater can eat more than 30,000 termites or ants a day!

# Tapir

The tapir is a large mammal, 6–8 feet long and about 440 pounds. Its nose and upper lip form a short trunk, which it uses to pluck fruit and plant to eat. Tapirs live near water and can often be seen wallowing in the mud.

The baby tapir has spots and stripes that help it hide in the dappled light of the fore The markings gradually disappear as the tapir grows bigger, stronger, and faster.

# Boa Constrictor

The boa constrictor is a large snake that can grow to 13 feet long. It is not poisonous, but it is a fearsome predator. It coils around a branch and patiently waits for prey to pass by. When a rodent or small mammal approaches, the boa lunges, grabs the animal with its mouth, then quickly coils around it in a tight hug until the animal suffocates. The boa swallows its prey whole, and then returns to its branch to slowly digest its meal.

# Poison Dart Frog

Unlike the huge boa, these tiny ½- to 2-inch frogs *are* poisonous! Their bright colors act as a warning, telling predators to keep away—because glands of poison dart frogs produce the world's most powerful animal poison, called *batracotoxin*. A fraction of an ounce of this venom can kill 4,000 people.

# Macaw

The Amazon rainforest is home to some amazingly colorful birds, including macaws—the largest parrots of the Americas. Macaws can grow to over 2 feet long (which includes its 15-inch tail). They come in a variety of bright colors from deep red, to emerald green, to vibrant blues.

In the morning, macaws leave their nests and meet in noisy groups on treetops to bask in the sun. They use their strong beaks to help them move from branch to branch. Later they drift away to the forest to look for food.

The nest is built in a hollow tree trunk, often quite high up. The parents defend the eggs from predators and will attack anything that goes near the nest.

## What does it eat?

Fruits, seeds, nuts, and insects. Macaws can crack even the hardest, largest shells with their strong beaks, and easily remove the nuts with their thick tongues.

# Quetzal

Quetzal
Toucan

The quetzal is one of the most beautiful birds of the rainforest of Central America. It is 14–16 inches long and has a very long tail, particularly the male.
The quetzal eats berries, fruits, tender shoots, insects, snails, lizards, and small frogs. Both male and female quetzals help build the nest and take turns sitting on the eggs.

## Toucan

The toucan is a large bird, 10–18 inches long, with an enormous (but lightweight) beak. The toucan can pick ripe fruit from trees with its beak—which is so long that the bird can reach berries on even the slimmest branches.
Toucans are cheerful, intelligent birds. They gather in noisy, playful flocks on treetops in the tropical forests.

Creature Feature:
The male quetzal is quite vain about his tail, which he uses to attract females. When he looks for food, he is careful not to get his tail tangled in the undergrowth.

Did You Know?
There are about 40 types of toucan, each with a different color beak!

# Amazon River

The Amazon River is the longest river in South America—it flows about 4,000 miles to the Atlantic Ocean. Many smaller rivers feed into the great Amazon on its way to the ocean. The waters in these rivers are brimming with life.

Of the hundreds of species of fish, the most famous fish is the piranha, known or its tiny sharp teeth. Here also live water mammals, such as the rare freshwater dolphin, and, at the river's mouth, the manatee, a peaceful animal that grazes on riverbed plants.

There are also incredible reptiles in the Amazon. The little basilisk lizard runs along the top of the water to escape predators like the bush dog and the giant otter. The caiman swims just below the surface, staying clear of the huge anaconda—a snake large enough to eat big mammals such as the capybara and the paca.

Bush Dog

Giant Otter

Arapaima

Piranha

12

Paca

Capybara

Anaconda

Spectacled Caiman

Basilisk

Manatee

Amazon River Dolphin

13

# Manatee

**Creature Feature:**
Peaceful, slow-moving manatees help small rivers to keep flowing smoothly by eating 55-65 pounds of water plants a day.

The manatee, or sea cow, is a large mammal of the walrus family. It is 10–13 feet long and weighs 1,100–1,300 pounds. It has gray, wrinkled skin, often encrusted with seaweed. It uses its flippers to move through the water and to hold onto food while it eats.

Baby manatees are about 3 feet long and weigh 33–45 pounds. The mother nurses her young on milk for more than a year, although young manatees begin to eat water plants when they are only a few weeks old. The mother takes care of her baby and protects it by wrapping her long flippers around it.

# Capybara

The capybara is the world's largest rodent. It is 3 to 4 feet long and weighs over 100 pounds! Wow! That's one big water rat! This mild-natured, shy animal prefers to run away rather than face a threat, but if it has no choice, it will defend itself bravely, biting back with its strong front teeth. The capybara lives in and near rivers and swamps, and is able to swim long distances underwater for many minutes. Young capybaras stay with their mother for a long time, going with her to look for food, learning to choose the best grass, and, above all, learning to defend themselves from many predators, such as the anaconda, the jaguar, and the caiman.

**What does it eat?**
Water plants, leaves, seeds, and sometimes the bark from young trees, using its long, strong teeth.

# Spectacled Caiman

This caiman lives along the banks of rivers, lakes, and swamps. It is a large reptile that grows up to 10 feet long and can weigh 650 pounds. The caiman has partly-webbed front feet that help it swim. It has two bony crests around its eyes that make it look as if it is wearing spectacles (eyeglasses). The spectacled caiman has only two predators: the jaguar and the anaconda.

# Piranha

This 7–12-inch fish is famous for its ferocity. Piranhas have a keen sense of smell and are attracted to the odor of blood. Traveling in large schools, they swarm around a wounded or dying animal and rip it to shreds in a matter of minutes with their powerful, saw-toothed jaws—leaving only the skeleton!

## Did You Know?

Native people use the sharp piranha teeth as arrow tips, and the jaws are made into scissors and razors.

The anaconda is one of the largest snakes in the world. Some anacondas grow up to 36 feet long—and some have been sighted that are even longer! The anaconda lives alone in the swamps or on riverbanks, spending much of its time coiled on low branches or deep in pond waters.

Like the boa, it is a constrictor. As prey approaches, the snake grabs the animal with its mouth and drags it into the water to suffocate it. It opens its mouth wide and swallows the prey whole. It eats large mammals, rodents, birds, fish, turtles, and even caimans up to 6–7 feet long!

# From the Pampas to Patagonia

Ovenbird

In those areas of South America where little rain falls, the vegetation is mainly grass and bushes. The flat, dry northern-central plains of Argentina are called the pampas. Just south of the pampas, stretching to South America's southernmost tip, is the rolling land of grass and brush called Patagonia.

The animals that live in these regions cannot hide easily in the grass. Those with the keenest senses and the swiftest reflexes are able to escape predators. The pampas deer has an excellent sense of smell. The Patagonian mara has sharp hearing. The rhea, a large bird that looks like an ostrich, has good eyesight and moves very fast. The elegant crested tinamou, on the other hand, is able to blend in with the color of the tall grass.

Other animals, such as viscachas, live in underground burrows, where they hide from predators like the maned wolf, the pampas gray fox, and the Patagonian weasel. The largest predator of the grasslands—feared by all—is the puma. Agile and powerful, its best weapon is its pounce. In one leap it can cover more than 55 feet!

Rhea

Puma

Burrowing Owl

Pampas Deer

Mara

Maned Wolf

Elegant Crested Tinamou

Pampas Gray Fox

Weasel

Viscacha

19

# Andes Cordillera

The Andes Cordillera is the longest chain of mountains on Earth, running 5000 miles from the warm Caribbean Sea along the Pacific coast, down to the frigid cold of Tierr del Fuego, the southernmost tip of South America.

Only the strongest, best-adapted animals are able to survive the high, dry regions of the Ande

Vicuna

Alpaca

Guana

Chinchilla

Condor

he animals of the camel family, the
uanaco, vicuna, alpaca, and the llama,
e covered in long, soft coats to protect
em from the cold. The chinchilla is also covered
soft fur. High overhead flies the largest vulture in
e world—the Andean condor. It is a combination
power and grace, capable of flying for hours
thout moving a wing, kept afloat by the
nd off the mountains.

Llama

21

# Llama

Just like the camel of Africa and Asia, the llama is a very important animal to the humans who raise them. The llama is a *domesticated* (tamed) guanaco (a wild mammal of the Andes) that serves as a pet and pack animal. It also is a source of wool.

Llamas are larger than the vicuna, the alpaca, and the wild guanaco. Llamas stand about 4–5 feet at the shoulder and can weigh up to 300 pounds. Females usually give birth to only one young at a time, and feed their young on milk.

Creature Feature:
Llamas sometimes make a humming sound. And when they are irritated, they spit!

# Guanaco

The guanaco, one of the biggest South American mammals of the wild, lives in the highest areas of the Andes Cordillera, from Peru to Tierra del Fuego. It stands 3–4 feet high at the shoulder and can reach 225 pounds. It has strong slender legs that can run 40 miles an hour—outrunning a puma! Guanacos are grazers, stopping to eat grass as they move from place to place. The whole herd will not graze at the same time. While some eat, others will remain on watch for predators.

## Did You Know?

The guanaco and the camel came from the same animals, millions of years ago! These ancient animals lived in North America. Some migrated to Asia and became the camel. Some migrated to South America and became the guanaco.

# Spectacled Bear

Up in the mountains of Columbia and Bolivia lives a fruit-eating bear. It is 4–6 feet long and can weigh 300 pounds. Its coat is dark brown to black, and the two yellowish rings around its eyes look like spectacles.

The spectacled bear is an agile climber. At times it spends the night in a tree between two branches, or in a nest built with the branches and leaves of trees.

■ Spectacled Bear
□ Chinchilla

# Chinchilla

The chinchilla, a member of the rodent family, has one of the softest coats of fur in the world. In the wild, the chinchilla lives in the high mountains of the Andes. Weighing only 1 to 2 pounds, this animal is very quick. It can dart and hide in cracks between rocks, where it also finds shelter from the cold nights. It eats the moss and lichen that grow on the rocks, and needs very little water to survive.

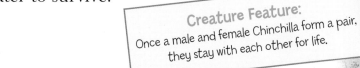

Creature Feature:
Once a male and female Chinchilla form a pair, they stay with each other for life.